DANGEROUS MAMMALS

HIPPOS

Madison Parker

NorwoodHouse Press

Library of Congress Cataloging-in-Publication Data:

Names: Parker, Madison.
Title: Hippos / Madison Parker.
Description: Buffalo, NY : Norwood House Press, 2025. | Series: Dangerous mammals | Includes glossary and index.
Identifiers: ISBN 9781684502653 (pbk.) | ISBN 9781684502660 (library bound) | ISBN 9781684502677 (ebook)
Subjects: LCSH: Hippopotamus--Juvenile literature.
Classification: LCC QL737.U57 P375 2025 | DDC 599.63'5--dc23

Published in 2025 by
Norwood House Press
2544 Clinton Street
Buffalo, NY 14224

Designer: Ocean Books
Editor: Kim Thompson

Photo credits: Cover, p. 1 Etienne Outram/Shutterstock.com; p. 5 Henk Bogard/Shutterstock.com; p. 6 Adwo/Shutterstock.com; p. 7 Baskoproducties/Shutterstock.com; p. 9 Photocechcz/Shutterstock.com; p. 11 Mikhail Semenov/Shutterstock.com; p. 13 Cheewin Blue/Shutterstock.com; p. 14 nwdph/Shutterstock.com; p. 17 Zsolt Biczo/Shutterstock.com; p. 18 Chedko/Shutterstock.com; p. 19 Claude Huolt/Shutterstock.com; p. 21 BlueOrange Studio/Shutterstock.com

Printed in the United States of America

CPSIA compliance information: Batch #CW25NHP: For further information contact Norwood House Press at 1-800-237-9932

TABLE OF CONTENTS

MEET THE HIPPO

Hippos are large animals. They live in water and on land. Hippos are **mammals**. Their babies drink milk.

TYPES OF HIPPOS

The common hippopotamus is also called the river hippopotamus or the Nile hippopotamus. These are all names for the same animal.

The common hippo is very large. It has a wide body, a huge mouth, and big teeth. It has thick skin and almost no hair. Its eyes and **nostrils** are on the top of its head.

Common hippos live in Africa near rivers and lakes. They sleep in the water to stay cool.

If they get upset, they can **charge** very fast. They can bite. They can tip over boats in the water. Hippos are most dangerous when they are protecting their babies.

The pygmy hippo is smaller and lighter than the common hippo. It is about half as tall as an adult human. This hippo has dark gray skin that is smooth and shiny.

Pygmy hippos live in western Africa. They like **dense** forests near rivers. They also live in swamps and **wetlands**.

Pygmy hippos are usually calm, but they can be dangerous. They have strong jaws and sharp teeth. If they feel **threatened**, they might bite.

FAVORITE FOODS

Hippos are mainly **herbivores**, or plant-eaters. They can eat 110 pounds (50 kilograms) of grass in one day.

Sometimes, hippos attack other animals for a meal. They will eat wildebeests, zebras, and kudu. They also steal meat from other **predators**.

For a sweet treat, hippos eat fruit that falls from trees. Hippos in zoos eat melons. Their powerful jaws easily break the fruit apart.

STAYING SAFE AROUND HIPPOS

If you see a hippo, stay far away. Hippos can move quickly on land and in water. It is safest to watch them from a distance.

Never stand between a hippo and water. They like to be able to get in the water. If they feel trapped, they may charge.

Stay inside a vehicle or on a boat to watch hippos. Keep quiet and move slowly. This helps you see them without scaring them.

GLOSSARY

charge (chahrj): to attack in a rush

dense (dens): crowded or thick

herbivores (HUR-buh-vorz): animals that eat only plants

mammals (MAM-uhlz): animals that are warm-blooded, that have hair or fur, that usually give birth to live babies, and that produce milk to feed their babies

nostrils (NAH-strulz): openings in the nose that animals breathe and smell through

predators (PRED-uh-turz): animals that live by hunting other animals for food

threatened (THRE-tuhnd): in danger of being harmed

wetlands (WET-landz): lands where there is a lot of moisture in the soil, including swamps and marshes

THINKING QUESTIONS

1. Why are hippos mammals?
2. What kinds of food do hippos like to eat?
3. What should you do if you see a hippo?
4. What are the differences between the common hippo and the pygmy hippo?
5. Where do hippos live?

INDEX

ABOUT THE AUTHOR

Madison Parker spent her childhood in the city of Chicago, Illinois. A farm girl at heart, today she lives in Wisconsin with her husband and four children on a small farm with cows, goats, chickens, and two miniature horses named Harley and David. Her favorite dessert is vanilla frozen custard with rainbow sprinkles, even in the winter.